I WANT TO BE A
DIVER

Written by
Jonathan Reule

Illustration
Carlos Varejão

Storyboard
Jonathan Reule & Shermaine See

UNIBINO
B O O K S

First paperback edition March 2023
ISBN 978-981-18-6521-3

Published by Unibino Pte. Ltd.
31 Rochester Drive Level 3, #03-47 Singapore 138637

www.unibino.com

All living things need water to survive. That is why we have built our societies around water sources for drinking and washing since the beginning of time.

These natural resources were essential for our survival. But being natural explorers, our curiosity nudged us to uncover what lurks beneath these large bodies of water.

For the most part, we could easily see the creatures living in shallower waters. Some of them fiercely protected their habitats, shooing humans away on sight! Others hid near the shores, waiting for the right time to strike unsuspecting prey.

For a long time, humans have both respected and feared the power of water. We stayed at the edge, just enough to collect the water we needed and avoided going any further. However, we never stopped being curious about what lay beyond our terrestrial borders and within those mysterious lakes, rivers, and seas.

Soon, we found ways to travel long distances over large bodies of water more safely. Boats kept us safe from most of the dangers underwater and allowed us to travel further out to sea to fish for food and even explore new lands.

As we began harvesting food from deeper waters, we discovered that there was an entirely different world underneath the surface. However, we could only hold our breath for so long before we had to return to the surface for air.

Some early civilisations such as the ancient Polynesians spent much of their time at sea. They were known for travelling far and wide over the oceans. This also made them incredibly skilled divers who could hold their breath for much longer than the average person. They would catch fish underwater and then eat them raw or with a little bit of salt.

For many centuries, this lifestyle kept the ancient Polynesians alive. Many were seafarers who travelled long distances over the sea and eventually settled around the Southeast Asian region. However, diving was not a profitable career then until much later.

Even as some of us developed increased lung capacity, there was still a limit to the amount of time we could stay underwater. Thus, people started experimenting with gadgets that could help us breathe while we swam underwater.

There are stories from the past about people who used hollow reeds as snorkelling devices, especially when they wanted to remain unseen.

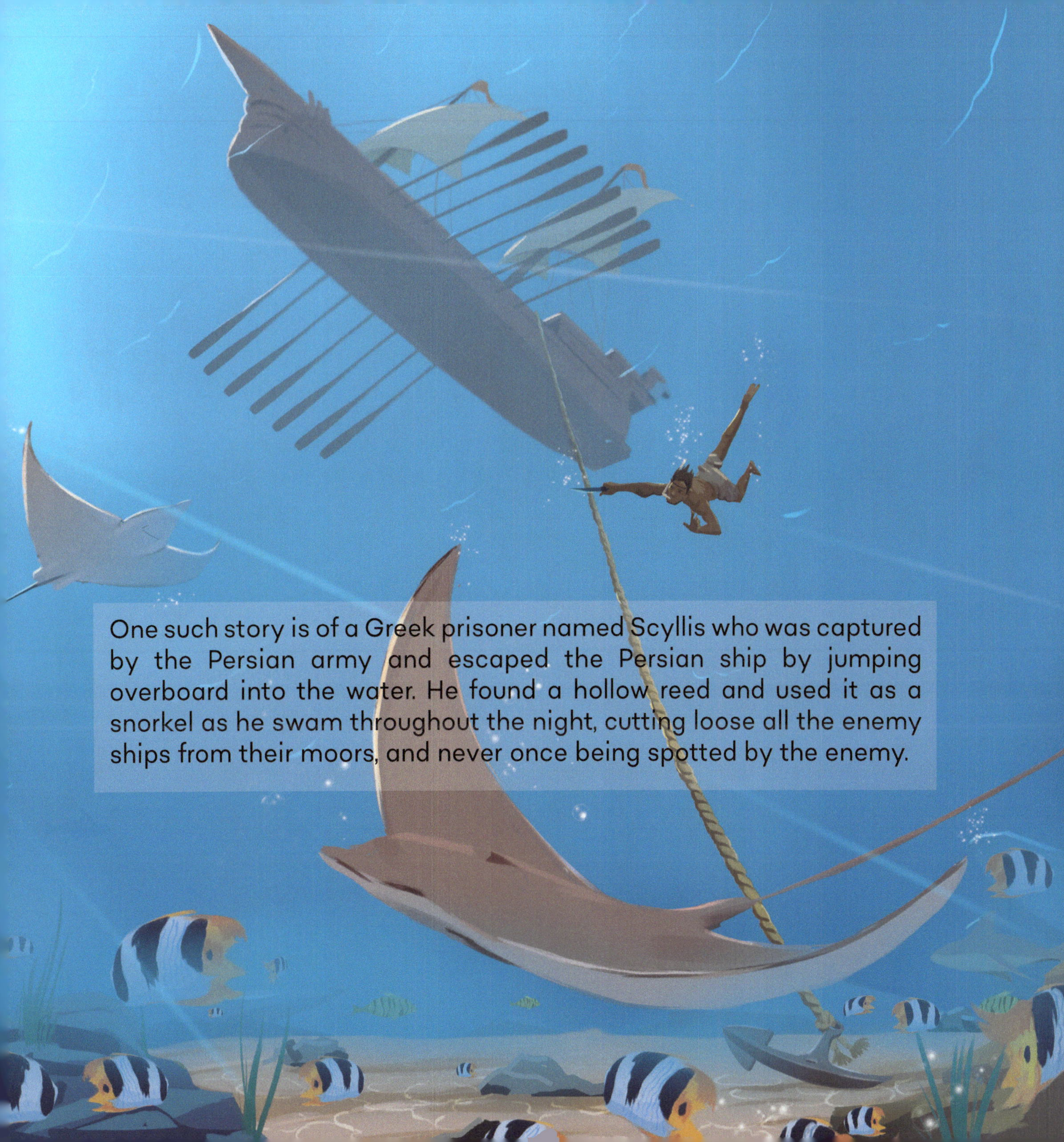

One such story is of a Greek prisoner named Scyllis who was captured by the Persian army and escaped the Persian ship by jumping overboard into the water. He found a hollow reed and used it as a snorkel as he swam throughout the night, cutting loose all the enemy ships from their moors, and never once being spotted by the enemy.

Aristotle also wrote about his pupil Alexander the Great being submerged underwater in a closed-up barrel where he remained dry and supplied with air for longer than any human could hold their breath. This tale has yet to be proven true, but the thought and design mentioned in the story were not far off from what inventors would create later on in our history.

More tales emerged from the 15th century about Greek warriors swimming underwater with air sacs so they can breathe from them without having to resurface before they were ready to attack. The ancient Persians were said to have made the first pair of goggles from polished turtle shells that gave them the ability to see underwater.

As diving tools became more readily available and adopted by people from all around the world, we began harvesting more resources from the water, and many of these early divers began using their diving skills to earn money. The Greeks were the first recorded civilisation to hire divers to collect underwater sponges that they would dry and sell on land.

Around the same time, Koreans from Jeju Island made a living from diving. These divers went underwater to collect seafood, such as molluscs, seaweed and other edibles. Initially, most of these divers were men, but by the 18th century, this profession was mostly dominated by women, also called Haenyeo, who have been known for collecting food in cold waters to sell at their local markets.

Soon, better technology helped us to stay underwater for longer than ever before. In the 1500s, an Italian inventor named Guglielmo de Lorena made what many consider to be the first modern diving bell. It was a device that was similar to what Alexander the Great was said to use, and it allowed divers to be submerged underwater while maintaining the ability to breathe.

The design of the diving bell was simple. It had a rope attached to its top, an air tube running through the chamber to keep oxygen fresh, and weights to help the diving bell sink. The bell would then be lowered into the water where it would remain dry on the inside, allowing divers to reach the bottom of the sea. Divers could then swim out from under the device to search old ship wreckages or pluck up sea clams and return to the bell to breathe in fresh air when they needed to.

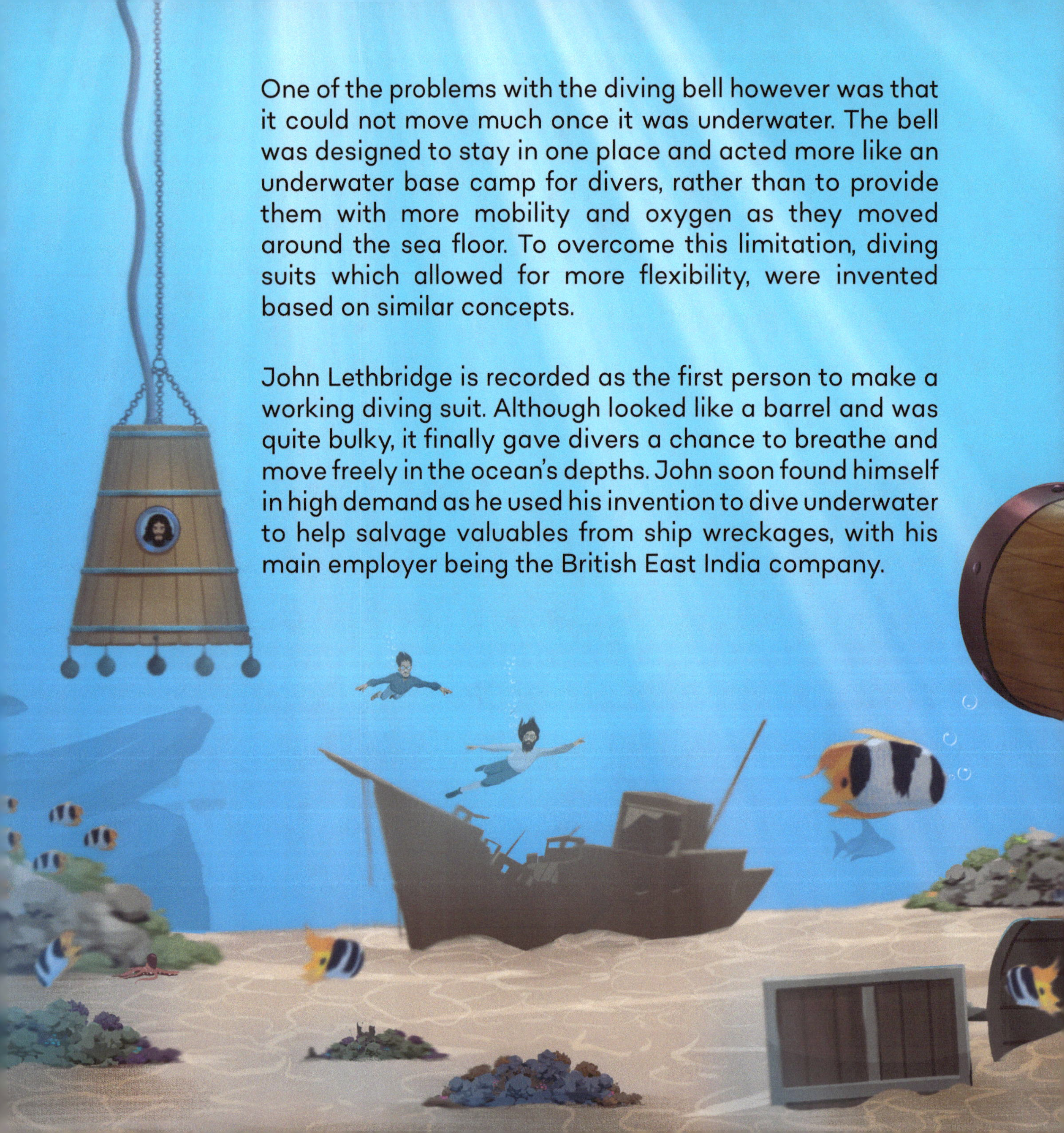

One of the problems with the diving bell however was that it could not move much once it was underwater. The bell was designed to stay in one place and acted more like an underwater base camp for divers, rather than to provide them with more mobility and oxygen as they moved around the sea floor. To overcome this limitation, diving suits which allowed for more flexibility, were invented based on similar concepts.

John Lethbridge is recorded as the first person to make a working diving suit. Although looked like a barrel and was quite bulky, it finally gave divers a chance to breathe and move freely in the ocean's depths. John soon found himself in high demand as he used his invention to dive underwater to help salvage valuables from ship wreckages, with his main employer being the British East India company.

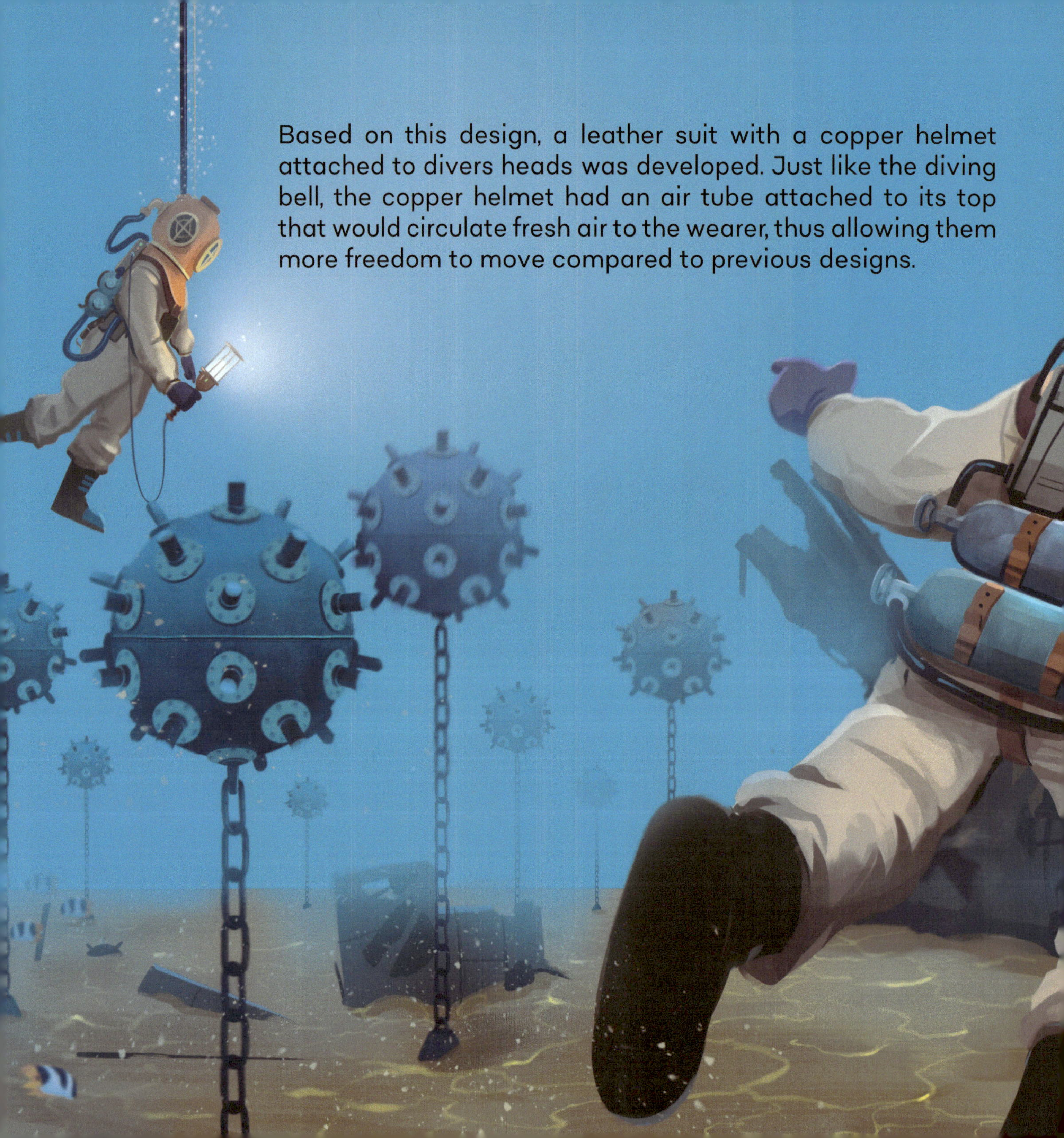

Based on this design, a leather suit with a copper helmet attached to divers heads was developed. Just like the diving bell, the copper helmet had an air tube attached to its top that would circulate fresh air to the wearer, thus allowing them more freedom to move compared to previous designs.

Such diving suits became pivotal for undersea excursions. They offered us the ability to walk underwater, see clearly through the glass fixed in the helmet, recycle air to keep us alive and explore underwater like never before. These diving suits were eventually equipped with communication devices, giving divers the ability to communicate with each other underwater and even with those above the surface.

Around this time, several engineers tried to design a self-contained underwater breathing apparatus (SCUBA) that would not be limited by a surface tube for its air supply. This led to the creation of gas canisters which could be taken underwater and used with a rebreather device for a period of time.

The rebreather came with several upgrades and advancements that eventually led us to what we have today. Modern SCUBA diving technology has expanded the areas and types of work that divers can do. So, what does it take to become a trained SCUBA diver?

It is important to be safe while diving underwater. It is even more important to know how to use the SCUBA gear properly so you will not be caught in a tight situation without any air supply. That's why all SCUBA divers have to undergo training before they can be certified as professionals.

SCUBA training normally consists of hours spent underwater with an instructor who will teach you the basics and other emergency procedures in case you encounter any danger during your dive. After receiving basic training, divers will be ready to apply what they learned in real-world professions.

The field of diving offers a wide range of opportunities for those interested in exploring the underwater world. For instance, diving instructors often take recreational divers, including tourists, on trips to explore the breathtaking underwater scenery and the fascinating sea creatures that inhabit it.

Divers who are passionate about photography can also work as underwater photographers. These professionals are not only divers but also artists. They take their cameras on dives to capture the best underwater scenes they can!

Divers are also in demand in the field of science. In particular, marine archaeologists often need to dive underwater to search the ruins of shipwrecks or the seabed to uncover items from the past. There are also marine biologists who may need to dive underwater to observe and study the different types of sea creatures. As a result, divers are not only explorers but also integral contributors to the advancement of scientific knowledge.

Aquariums also employ divers for maintenance and cleaning tasks to ensure the well-being of the aquatic life in their tanks. These divers use specialized equipment and techniques to clean and repair tanks, monitor water quality, and care for the animals living inside them. It's a crucial job to maintain a safe and healthy environment for the creatures and to keep the aquarium running smoothly.

Public safety divers are always on call. Whether it is day or night, these trained individuals are ready to gear up and help out in emergencies when called upon. For example, public safety divers may be called to explore a crime scene in murky waters that give them little to no visibility!

The military also employs divers to carry out a wide range of tasks. From search and rescue missions to disposing of sea mines before they explode, military divers need to be in great shape and have a sharp mind so they can focus clearly while underwater.

These are not the only places that hire divers. There are plenty of other places where Divers are necessary. Oil rigs need divers to help with underwater pipes. Golf courses need divers to help retrieve misfired balls from lakes and ponds around their courses.

As you can see, diving has served us for a long time in the past and will continue to do so in the future. If you're keen on swimming and exploring what lies beneath the water's surface, then maybe diving might be the right profession for you.

My Inspiration

Shubhi Saxena
Founder, Unibino

As a parent in this ever-changing world, it can sometimes feel overwhelming when it comes to our children's futures. New technologies seem to be arising almost every day, and with so many innovations, it creates unique professions which many of us wouldn't have dreamed to be necessary only a few years ago. Which to me is a good thing. Because with so much variety, my children can have the opportunity to pick a career that will fit their personalities and build upon their strengths. As you may imagine, this desire within me to provide my children with the resources they needed to thrive, led me to search out books that would be easy enough for them to understand while teaching them about various professions.

Only, I found that these books were few and far between. Even if I could find a book about a certain profession geared towards young readers, I found them sparse inside and limited to only certain careers that may not fit my children's abilities. This is when I came up with the idea to write my own children's books, teaching them about all the various careers in the modern world. After months of researching different professions and learning more than I ever expected, I quickly realised this was going to be a bigger project than I first anticipated. I dove into the histories of these professions, discovering links to the past, and why these professions were now so important.

Ultimately my goal was to offer my children options, to show them that there is no one set path for everyone. But in this, I stumbled upon something bigger. I wanted to share this with future generations. To share with all children and parents about these careers, to help spark curiosity, and to instil a passion for the future. Everyone has special talents and abilities, and I hope that this series will be able to offer clarity and inspiration to children around the world. Because at the end of the day, it's never too early to start dreaming and never too late to take action. With this, I hope you enjoy this series and that your young ones become the best versions of themselves as they can achieve.

www.ingramcontent.com/pod-product-compliance
Lightning Source LLC
Chambersburg PA
CBHW042011110726
48006CB00004B/1042